The Maori

photographs
GORDON ELL

compiled by
PITA GRAHAM

**HERITAGE OF
NEW ZEALAND**

**THE BUSH PRESS
OF AUCKLAND**

Contents

The First New Zealanders 2
Living Off The Land 6
The Maori as Gardener 10
Maori Pa & Settlements 14
Maori Life and Spirit 19
Living in a Maori Pa 23
Ancient Treasures 26
Classic Maori Art 30
Clothes and Fabrics 34
Moko or Tattoo 36
Maori Ornament 37
Tribes and Their Canoes 39
Aotearoa — Isolated World 40

Illustrations

Ancient Campsites 5
Cave Drawings 8
Tool Quarry 9
Maori Gardens & Crops 11-13
Pa Sites 16-17, 20-21, 24
Archaic Artefacts 25-27
Classic Maori Art 28-30
Weaving and Fabric 32-33
Maori Ornaments 36

The First New Zealanders

The islands of New Zealand are remote from the rest of the world. The first settlers reached these shores not much more than 1000 years ago. They were Polynesian people from the tropical Pacific.

While people built cities on the great continents, New Zealand lay undiscovered on the edge of the great Pacific ocean. As civilisations rose and fell, few took the path towards the Pacific. Except for a people, beginning perhaps in Asia, who over thousands of years began to drift down the archipelagos and islands, towards the east. At some time, about 300 A.D. they spread towards the islands of eastern Polynesia. It is from these adventurers and survivors that the Maori people sprang.

At a time when European explorers feared, lest they sail over the edge of the world, the Polynesians were sailing over their horizons in double-hulled canoes. The giant canoes, perhaps 20 metres long and joined by a raft and shelter, could sail over a thousand kilometres carrying men, women and food. In such vessels the Polynesians reached and settled islands such as the Cook groups, spreading further into the unknown to claim Hawaii, the Society Islands, Easter Island, and eventually New Zealand. Here in the land of the long white cloud, Aotearoa, they found a colder climate and a different world from the tropical Pacific. In their struggle to survive on an hostile shore, the first Polynesians were bound to find a new way of life. In doing so they developed a new culture, known today as Maori.

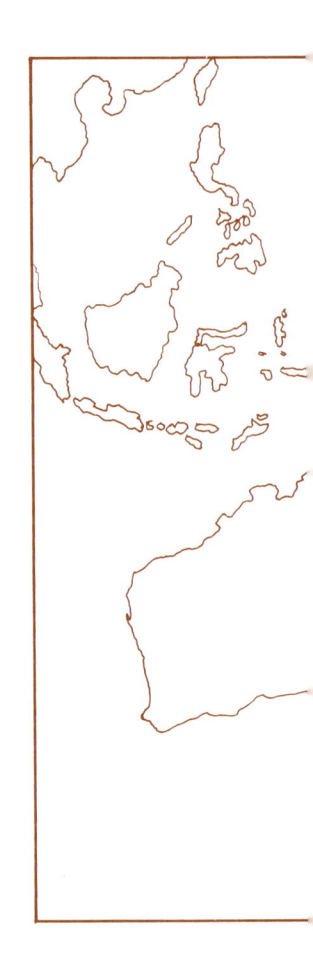

The exact date when Polynesians reached these islands is unknown but times about 850 A.D. are suggested. The fact is that some time about the ninth century some Polynesian people from the tropical Pacific landed on these temperate shores and learnt to live here.

The evidence of their struggle can still be found today about the coasts and harbours of New Zealand. It takes the form of campfires and burials, broken tools and the bones of animals they ate. Scientists, testing these remains, have been able to establish dates for these early "settlements". By using a process called Carbon-14 dating, they are able to work out when an animal or plant was killed or eaten. The process is approximate, accurate perhaps within 125 years, but it has helped to put dates on the sites of early Maori life.

A map of New Zealand showing where people lived about 1100 A.D. shows signs of settlement along the east coast of both North and South Islands. From this extent of population it is possible to work back and "guess" when the forefathers of these people may have come. By exploring the sites of early camps

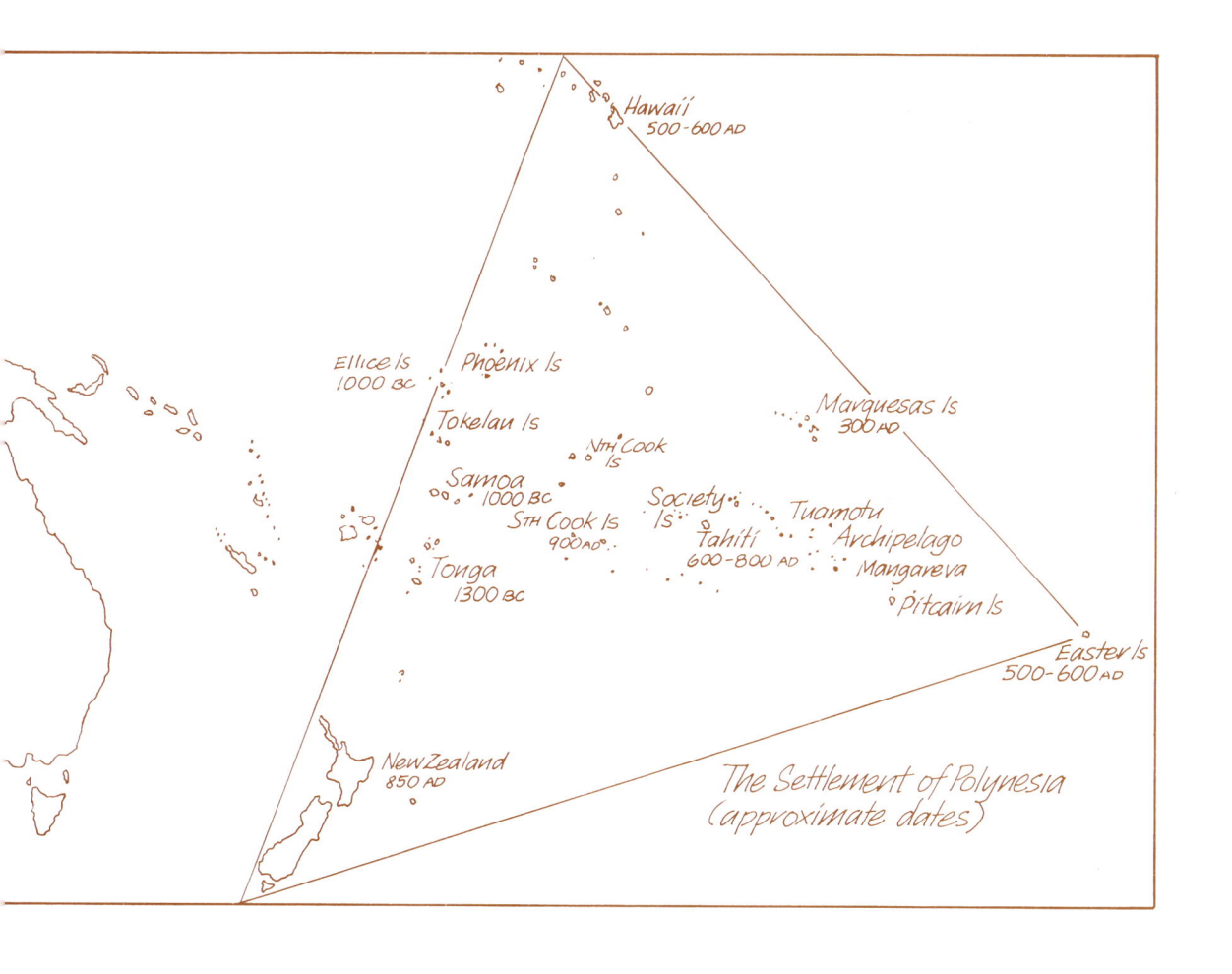

The Islands of Polynesia
The Maori people came from the tropical Pacific. They are Polynesians, a people who spread through the south-west Pacific, from about the time of Christ. Gradually they moved further into the Pacific, on double-hulled canoes, to occupy the islands in the region now known as the Polynesian triangle. Dates are from estimates in Peter Bellwood's *Man's Conquest of the Pacific*.

about the coasts of northern New Zealand it has been possible to find even earlier evidence, some dating back to around 900 A.D. The idea of settlement, perhaps in the early ninth century, is also helped by scientific work in the other islands of the South Pacific. This has given some suggestions about when the ancestors were moving into the region.

The islands of Aotearoa were unlike any the Polynesians had found before. They were large, rugged and densely grown with forests and swamps. The land was much colder than the little tropical islands they were used to. Most of the tropical vegetables they liked could not be grown and the animals and birds were different. Nevertheless the Polynesians were used to living off the land and they discovered new foods and ways to survive.

If the forests were dense they, at least, held millions of birds and these were often easy to catch. In the absence of any people many of the ancient birds survived, creatures like the moa and others which were flightless, or nearly so. The sea was rich in fish and the harbours and coasts yielded shellfish. The Polynesians were used to this diet and they used hooks to catch the fish just as they did at home. Such old hooks and lures, made from bone and shell, are so like those of other Pacific islands that it helps to prove those first New Zealanders were Polynesians.

Other clues which link the Maori with their Polynesian forefathers lie in the languages they speak. When Captain Cook explored New Zealand he brought with him a chief of Tahiti, Tupaea, who spoke a similar language to Maori, and acted as translator. The people of the Polynesian islands also have similar legends. They share folk traditions of people like Maui who fished up the land and the gods of sky, sea and forest. Their bone structure and burial customs are similar.

In their first campsites about Aotearoa the Polynesians left tools and ornaments that look the same as those made at that time in the other Polynesian islands. The development of Maori art and culture only began as the Polynesians discovered new ways to survive in this different and difficult land.

Clues to an ancient way of life. Rubbish gleaned from a campsite on the Coromandel Peninsula shows some of the food popular with early Polynesian settlers. The material from midden shown on next page, includes moa bone, skull of a kiore or Polynesian rat, and bush snail shells. Fragments of volcanic glass and chert provided tools for cutting, skinning and drilling.

Midden
Wind has eroded this sandhill at Port Jackson, Coromandel to reveal a midden, or rubbish heap, deposited centuries go by early Maori. Shells, bones and stone from fireplaces can be seen.

Ancient Campsites

Fireplace
Fat, from food cooked here, generations ago, has held together this fireplace in the sand dunes at Spirits Bay, Northland. Wind erosion of the sandhills reveals such sites from time to time.

SKELETONS OF A MOA AND A MAORI.

Living off the land

To the Polynesian, of the tropical Pacific, the cooler climate of New Zealand was a hostile place. Not only was the atmosphere much colder but many of the traditional foods could not be grown or gathered. On the other hand the deep forests and swamps provided different fare in the form of many birds, particularly the moa.

These giant flightless birds occurred in many parts of the country. The smallest may have been a metre high, the larger ones perhaps two or three metres. The leg bones of the largest stand higher than a man. Over a period of perhaps 300 to 400 years the Polynesians hunted the moa, and a number of other flightless birds, which are now extinct. The discovery of moa bones in the fireplaces of the first settlers shows how valuable the birds were for food.

The settlers hunted other creatures however, particularly the seal, tuatara, and a number of forest birds no longer found in great reaches of the country. Bones and black greasy fireplaces show they caught fish. They also ate insects and earthworms.

The Polynesians learned what fruit and roots to eat and the medicinal uses of bark and vegetation. Gradually they came to understand the nature of their new land and how it could be used for survival.

It is likely that the first Maori people moved about the countryside with the seasons. In this way they could take advantage of fruiting and growing seasons and also the seasonal movement of birds and fish. For example at times there were migratory birds, like the godwit, to net along the shores of the great harbours. These birds spend the summer in New Zealand but breed in Siberia more than 12,000 km away. Again there are seasons when the "muttonbirds" breed on the mountain peaks and offshore islands. Then their fat chicks were taken for food. Such seasonal hunting remained a part of Maori life when, in later centuries, the tribes began to settle about their defended villages or pa.

Looking through the rubbish dumps, or middens, left by the earliest Maori it is possible to see the remains of some of their meals. Shells, particularly, show how difficult it must have been to get a meal. Some are tiny, providing only a morsel, to be picked from a snail-like shell. The teeth of the settlers were swiftly worn down by the quantities of sand they ate, accidentally, with their food. Without teeth and on an unbalanced diet their lives were short.

Yet the settlers developed ways of preserving food for difficult times. Much of the fish catch, and birds too, were preserved. Birds could be kept in their own fat. Fish too can be kept after drying in the sun. Such techniques have been kept alive over the centuries and are still used in some districts.

Fern root was a frequent food. This was grubbed from the fields of bracken fern which grows on cleared forest land. The roots were beaten and cooked. Similar sugars were gathered by burning the roots of cabbage trees.

In some places a regular source of food encouraged settlement. Seal colonies about the coasts were much more widespread then. A tribal group, living close to a colony of seals, had a ready source of food and skins for clothing. The northern harbours with their rich resources of fish and shellfish were also attractive places to settle.

In a few favoured corners of the north some of the tropical plants brought to New Zealand by the Polynesians could survive. Thus stocks of kumara (sweet potato), taro, yams, gourds and tropical cabbage tree were kept alive.

As settlement spread efforts were made to take these popular foods further south. Frosts, however, killed the tropical plants and limited their natural range. Thus the population of Maori New Zealand probably grew largest in the north where the weather was warmer, frosts infrequent, and more food could be grown.

Cave Drawings

This rock shelter at Waipara in North Canterbury is a typical camp site of early Maori hunters. On the walls and ceiling are ochre and charcoal drawings done by the hunters. Some of these drawings have been retouched; the fainter marks are more typical of early cave drawings.

Tool Quarry

The roughly-outlined adzes shown above were left by their Maori makers on the floor of a rock quarry on the Coromandel Peninsula. Adzes of this type, dating back to the twelfth century, have been found in sites all about the eastern coast of New Zealand. Tools were made in the quarry (bottom left) and traded through the country. Large stones were used to break up basalt blocks then adzes were shaped with hammer stones (bottom right).

The Maori as Gardener

There are places in New Zealand where it is still possible to see the remains of ancient Maori gardens believed to date back 1000 years. Lines of stones and stone heaps mark areas where Maori people once grew kumara (the sweet potato), yams and gourds. Patches of wild taro growing in wet places and plantations of flax and karaka trees are other signs of the Maori as a gardener.

The original settlers from Polynesia were a people who combined fishing and hunting with extensive gardens. In the tropics they grew not only sweet potato but breadfruit, banana, yams and coconuts. Few of the tropical foods would grow in New Zealand's colder climate and those that did would only grow year round in the frost-free places farthest north. So it was that the first settlers relied more on hunting and gathering food from coastline and forest than they did on gardening. Yet that tradition was not lost and in a few favoured corners the old ways of agriculture were kept alive.

There are places in the north where traditions of gardening go back a very long way. On the Taiamai Plain behind the Bay of Islands there are signs of extensive gardens in piles and rows of rocks which still clutter the fertile soils below the volcanic pa sites. On the Coromandel Peninsula, on off-shore islands like Great Mercury nearby, and about some volcanic cones in Auckland there is further evidence of very early settlement and gardens. There, lines of stones may mark the borders of gardens where kumara were grown. The shelter they created, and the warmth generated by piles of stones, could allow a tropical crop like gourd or yam to grow to maturity despite the temperate climate.

The sweet potato, *Ipomoea batatas*, is a staple food in many tropical regions but in New Zealand it grows at the extreme limits of its range. Over the centuries the Maori people developed ways to raise the kumara in places further south and to keep its seed viable through the seasons of killing frost. To do this they invented a kind of underground storehouse. Dug a metre or more into the ground and roofed in totara bark, the kumara storepit maintained an even temperature through the winter. Safe inside the seed crop stayed alive until spring. These storepits left a distinctive mark on the landscape and their remains are known today as kumara pits. They can be seen about most Maori pa sites and near old garden areas. With their roofs gone and their sides broken in by stock, the kumara pits can still be traced as oblong hollows on the land.

Other signs of Maori gardens can be found in the nature of the soil itself. In many parts of northern New Zealand the modern gardener may find patches in the soil where Maori people have mixed in shell, or sand, to make the earth better for kumara.

Ko or Spade
to dig fern root & kumara

This stone pile, being excavated at Wiri in Auckland, reflected sun's heat for sensitive crops — like gourds — to grow in cooler climates of New Zealand. More garden pictures may be seen on the next two pages.

Maori people also planted certain trees in groves to provide them with food. Like orchards these trees produced fruit or roots which made suitable food. The tropical cabbage tree *Cordyline terminalis* is extinct in mainland New Zealand now but was once grown for its sugary roots. In colder districts the roots of the common cabbage tree *Cordyline australis* were dug out and eaten after cooking to extract the sugar. The fruit of the karaka tree was used, in various ways, after specially treating the highly-poisonous kernel. Plantings of this tree often mark ancient gardens and settlements. Taro was grown in swamps and along slow-moving creeks in the North. Flax plantations were the source of material for ropes, mats and other fabrics.

As Maori gardens developed the life style became more settled. Hunting and fishing parties still departed with the season to catch birds and fish and to forage for the natural foods of the forest — fruit, roots and leaves. The kumara, however, gave them a staple food. This helped the wandering Polynesians to settle in a particular place and establish a claim to that territory.

The importance of gardens varied in different parts of the country. In some places the hunting of seals and birds remained important while others depended more on fish from river or sea, or on digging fern root.

By the time the first European observers arrived there appeared to be two ways of life common in New Zealand. In warmer districts the Maori grew crops like the kumara and also went fishing, hunting and gathering foods in season. In the colder South Island the Maori depended more on moving with the seasons in search of food. The introduction of the potato, by the European discoverers, enabled the tribes further South to grow gardens and live a more settled life.

Above: Stone rows on a hillside at Great Mercury Island indicate where Maori people once grew their crops.
Below: Remains of a kumara store revealed on a pa site at Mimiwhangata, Northland. Pit was once deeper and roofed for protection from weather.

Maori Gardens and Foods

The remains of Maori gardens may still be seen today in places where the surface has not been disturbed by farming or forestry.

Taro plant on right was photographed in Northland some kilometres from present settlement. Taro is still a popular crop in some warmer districts though modern varieties have replaced the original tropical strain introduced by the Polynesians.

Karaka trees were often planted about Maori pa and settlements. Their golden fruit has a highly-poisonous kernel. Plantations of flax were also grown by Maori gardeners, as were tropical cabbage trees, now extinct in the wild.

Maori pa and settlements

The rich gardens of a Maori settlement were a target for enemies. Food was often in short supply and the existence of a neighbour's store of kumara led to many raids. The season for Maori warfare was winter when the crops were gathered in and housed in the kumara pits.

Hungry tribes then sent warriors on the trail to rob their more fortunate neighbours. Not surprisingly the tribes which grew crops developed a system of protecting them. The fortresses they built are known today as fighting pa.

Maori pa can still be seen as ruins about the countryside of New Zealand. There are more than 5500 recorded in the North Island and perhaps 100 or so in the South Island. Maori pa are more often found in warmer areas for these are where the Maori had their kumara gardens for centuries.

The ruins of a Maori pa often show a system of terraces, or ditches and banks, about a headland or small hill. Many are close to the sea for the Maori still drew much of their food from fish, shellfish and seabirds. More pa are to be found inland along the courses of rivers which once served as roads to the interior. These pa may have relied on local gardens, the natural riches of the forest, and the native fish and eels which inhabited the rivers and lakes. Usually the pa near the coast were established first, then new pa inland were developed as coastal population grew and succeeding generations moved inland.

Maori pa are designed for easy defence. Often they are surrounded by sea cliffs or steep ridges to help keep out enemies. A wall of upright logs, built across the neck of a headland, kept out enemies approaching from inland.

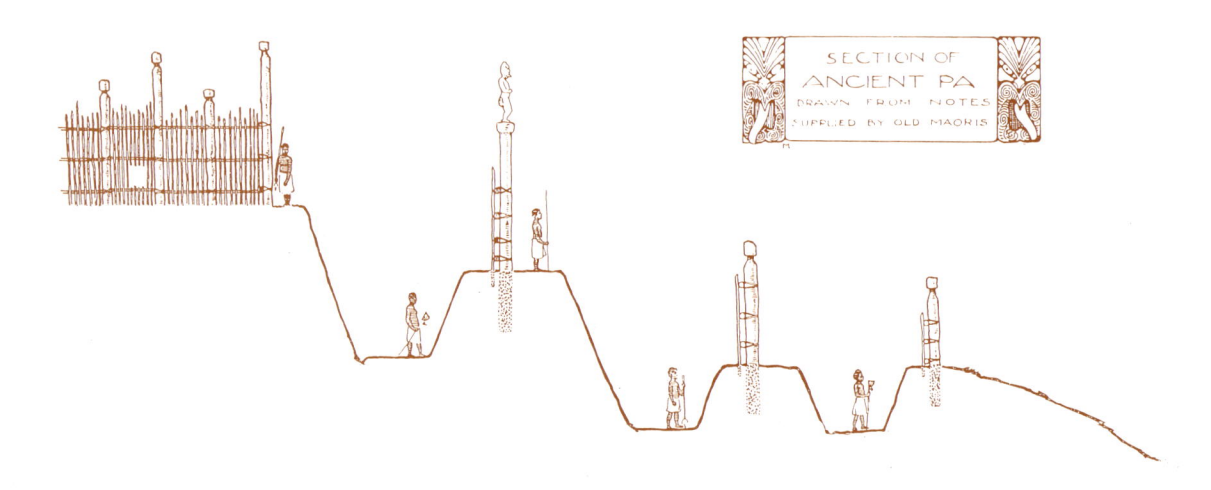

SECTION OF ANCIENT PA
DRAWN FROM NOTES SUPPLIED BY OLD MAORIS

In other cases a whole hill might be fortified. The small volcanoes of Auckland and Northland often show signs of once being the site of Maori pa. Terraces around their slopes may mark where houses stood. On the outer edge of the terraces, palisades of logs were built as a defence against attackers. In other places ditches and banks were dug, adding to the height of the palisades.

Any enemy wanting to attack would have to fight his way over walls the height of tree trunks, or capture a narrow gate, in hand-to-hand fighting. More often the pa could not be broken into so the attackers resorted to some trickery, such as a false truce, to get their enemy into the open outside the walls. In other cases the enemy got into the pa by pretending friendship then murdered their hosts in the night.

The Maori fought for food and also for hunting and fishing places. Often the pa commanded not only gardens but fine fisheries as well. The pa that had a harbour full of fish and shellfish, beside its garden, was rich indeed. For this reason a particularly fine harbour may have several pa sites about its rim.

Sometimes, as gardens lost their fertility, the Maori people moved to another pa nearby. In any case many of the ordinary people lived outside the pa, close to the gardens. It was only when the war chant and the shell bugle warned of attack, that the ordinary people withdrew behind the walls of their pa.

Some pa were very large. It is estimated that perhaps 1000 people lived on the slopes of One Tree Hill (Maungakiekie) or Mount Eden (Maungawhau) when population was heaviest on the shores of Auckland. Other pa were quite small, perhaps outliers of larger settlements, or simply refuges for women and children when under attack. Sometimes a little offshore rock might become a refuge, the people scrambling up rope ladders, then pulling the ropes up after them so they could not be reached by the enemy.

Other pa stood along the borders between two Maori tribes. Such lines of pa can still be seen on the hills which separate tribal areas today. Along the summit of the Papamoa Hills, between Tauranga and Rotorua peoples, there are fortifications extending several kilometres to mark where the tribal boundaries were once contested.

During the course of a year a tribal group might use a number of pa, moving about with seasonal activities, such as catching birds and fish.

Some Maori pa are very ancient. Settlement of parts of the Auckland isthmus have been traced back to around the twelfth century while an even longer history is now being revealed in the Bay of Islands. Maori traditions recount the battles for many of these places, fought by the tribes which survive today. Archaeological excavations have, however, revealed even older settlements buried in the earth below the existing pa.

Maori Pa

Hillsides marked with terraces like this are a feature of many North Island districts. These are the remains of Maori pa, or forts. Once the outer edge of the terraces held walls of upright logs, or palisades. There are more than 5500 recorded pa sites in the North Island and a further 100 or so in the South Island. The people who lived nearby withdrew into the pa when enemies arrived. The picture (left) looks up the ridge of the pa shown in profile above. On right are two pa built on volcanic hills: top Bay of Islands, below Mt Eden (Maungawhau) in Auckland. Note remains of kumara pit near summit or tihi.

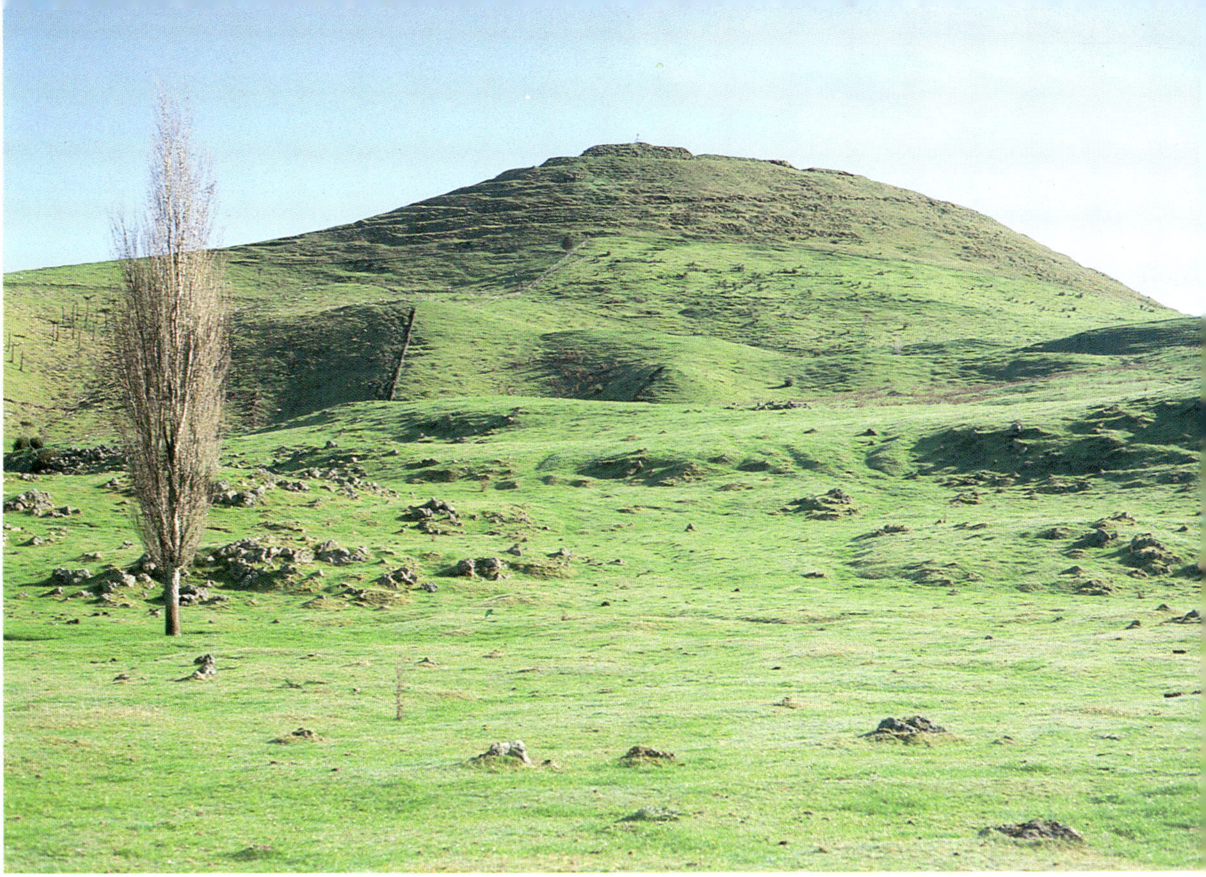

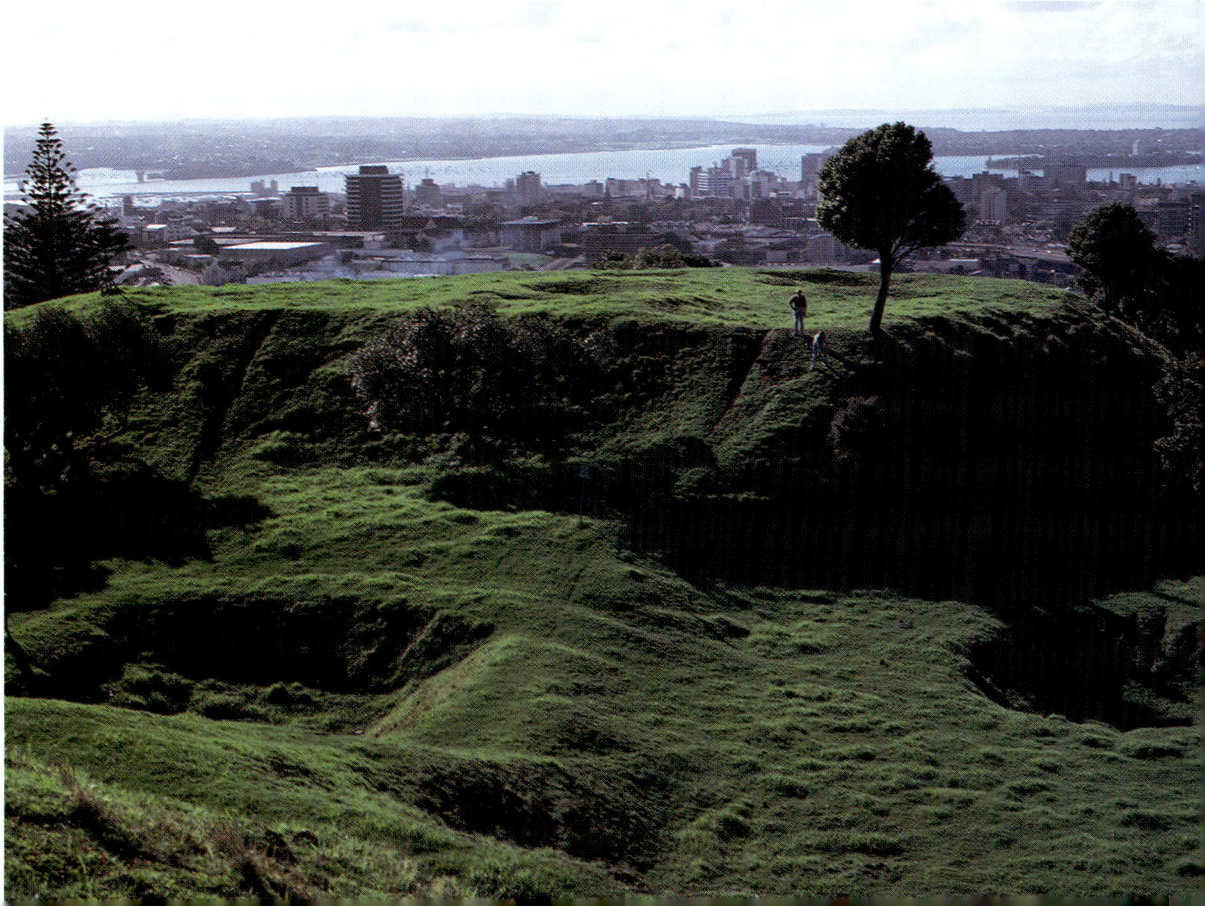

MAORI LIFE – Villages and their people

The undefended villages, kainga, have left little mark on the landscape. Simple huts, surrounded by brushwood walls, made up such a village and there were no defensive banks or ditches. When attacked the occupants of the kainga might retire to a nearby fortified village with other members of their tribe.

The Maori tribe, or iwi, might hold a considerable tract of country through its various branches. This included control of forests and fisheries, by hunting and fishing rights. As the tribe grew through the generations new sub-tribes, or hapu, might be set up when a family moved away from the first settlement and occupied its own corner of the territory. The Tainui tribes, for example, moved inland from Kawhia over the generations, to occupy the valleys of Waikato.

The basic group within the tribe however was the family, or whanau. This was a wider grouping than the European family, covering three or four generations of relationship, all working together. Such a whanau had its own land to work and tasks within the hapu.

Men did those jobs which involved tapu, the sacredness surrounding the building of canoes and planting of crops, for example. There were many chiefs, or elders of families, who took part in the decisions of tribal life.

The warriors were also the hunters with their special skills and tools, knowledgeable about the countryside and the places to secure its creatures.

The higher-born women were responsible for the practice of crafts like weaving and plaiting, the making of fabrics. Women too had the tasks of tending the gardens and gathering wild plants and firewood.

Cooking was a task for women only.

Sometimes men and women worked together perhaps in the preparation of fields. Yet only men fished the sea, while the women gathered shellfish. Carving was the job of special men.

A class of tohunga priests foretold the future and set the timetables for planting and harvest. Schools, or whare wananga, prepared young men for lives as warriors or priests.

Menial tasks and jobs beyond the pale of tapu or sacred persons were performed by a slave class. Slaves were usually captives of other tribes or subject people, whose mana and tapu were less.

WAIRUA – the spirit world

To survive the Maori had to live with nature not fight against it. The intimacy between people and the land was therefore deep. Atua, or gods, protected everything. Tangaroa, for example, protected the ocean and all the life within it. Tane was the protector of the forest and its creatures. These spirits dwelt in the land and to disturb their offspring, for example to catch a fish or fell a tree, demanded first a karakia or incantation. Such karakia attended every aspect of Maori life, for the world, and all living things, are part of one whole.

These figures also gave a "human shape" to the elements and natural phenomena, like wind and fire, the rainbow and the thunder. They occur in story as people and in substance as parts of the natural world – the remnants of fire sprung from Mahuika's fingers took refuge from the rain and sheltered in the body of the maiden Hine kaikomako. It was by rubbing together sticks of the kaikomako tree, that the Maori generated fire.

Mahuika, with fingernails of fire. Legend tells of Maui plucking the fires, one by one. Picture from W Dittmer's Te Tohunga.

TAPU – protecting the spirit

The Maori adapted the traditions of their Pacific homeland to the new landscape. The gods of forest and sea, earth and sky, gave reason and order to the new plants and animals of Aotearoa. Traditions to respect and harbour these resources became part of ritual life.

Everything had its season and its purpose. The right karakia were recited to encourage the crop or the catch. Rahui protected fishery and forest from over-exploitation. A complex of tapu surrounded many aspects of life.

Tapu, a kind of sacred protection, could be laid upon a person or a place; perhaps following a death, or to protect a tree or spirit. Tapu protected the processes of agriculture and construction. Karakia, to placate the atua spirit in things, were continually recited before even simple tasks like disposing of nail clippings and hair. Such practices continue to this day. The head was particularly tapu and even the whole persons of certain high chiefs.

The system of tapu served to guide Maori people much as the law does for Europeans: fear of breaking a tapu acted as a form of discipline. A broken tapu could lead to a loss of protection from the offended atua; an invitation to disaster and death.

Above: Ditches and banks formed additional obstacles when warriors attacked these pa. Ditches were once much deeper and palisades stood on their banks.

Below: Midden, or rubbish tip, of shell exposed by erosion of a pa site.

20

Signs of the Maori Past

These views of Maori pa show some of the easier-to-recognise features. Ditches and banks were sometimes built to give added protection to the pa. Palisades of logs stood on the banks overlooking the ditches, making attack difficult. One Tree Hill (Maungakiekie), top left and right, is a volcano with several defensive positions about its rim. Middens of shells often occur about pa sites, the rubbish tips of meals eaten long ago.

Living in a Maori Pa

While paintings of the nineteenth century often show Maori houses with fine carvings on their face, most of the people lived in huts made of brushwood and thatched with bulrush, nikau leaves or totara bark. The large meeting houses, finely carved, were also a nineteenth century development produced with steel tools.

The ancient Maori lived in tiny huts. The walls were low and to enter such houses meant bending double or crawling. A fireplace inside served to give some warmth and discourage insects. The people indoors slept on fern beds and mats. The chief's house was usually the largest and best constructed.

Such houses leave few marks on the landscape. Usually their position is found by looking for flat areas within the banks of an abandoned pa. When excavated they usually reveal only the position of a few post holes and the burnt stones of a fireplace. In some places the houses were sunken for extra protection from winds and cold.

RECONSTRUCTED MAORI PA
At Rewa's village, Kerikeri, tourists can see how the Maori once lived. Houses were tiny, often enclosed by stakes. Cooking was done in a separate shelter. Chief lived in larger house on tihi, top of pa.

Cooking, a process surrounded by tapu, was done in a separate shelter. Often food was cooked in underground ovens called hangi. Heated stones were made to steam by the use of water and green leaves to wrap the food in. Much of the food, however, was eaten raw. The middens of rubbish dumped from the pa reveals some of the diet in shells, fish bones, dog bones, and the skeletons of creatures like the kiore or Polynesian rat and various birds.

Dogs and kiore were brought to New Zealand by the Polynesians. Dogs may have been used to hunt ground-nesting birds. They also provided food and a source of skins for cloaks. The existence of these introduced mammals led to the building of storehouses on poles. Such pataka kept supplies safe and dry above ground. Other structures on tall poles might carry the bones of a high-born person prior to burial, or tribal treasures in the form of greenstone.

These pictures show a reconstructed village of pre-European times built at Kerikeri, Bay of Islands by the Society for the Preservation of the Stone Store Area, an historic place nearby.

Maori Pa

**MAORI PA
IN 1844**
While European contact was well-established by this time paintings by George French Angas, indicate the appearance of Maori settlement, including defensive walls of pa. These paintings are of Motupoi Pa, in the shade of the Tongariro volcanoes of the central North Island, at Lake Rotoaira.

These tools and ornaments date from early times when the islands of eastern Polynesia still shared a common culture. Later Polynesian settlers of New Zealand developed a distinctive Maori style, more highly decorated (See Classic Maori Art).

The first settler had to change the materials they worked in, to reproduce their traditional artefacts, in New Zealand. The breast decoration at top, for example, was originally made of pearl shell. In New Zealand there is no pearl shell but the same shape is worked from stone.

The fishing lures on the left of the display stand also show this change. One is made with tropical pearl shell, the lower one from paua, a highly-coloured shell found about the New Zealand coast. Other fish hooks show similar forms from several Pacific islands, each made with locally-available material.

Archaic Tools and Ornament

The adzes below are of types popular with the Eastern Polynesian people. While they look similar, only the second and fourth adzes (from left) were made in New Zealand. Similar forms from other islands help define a culture, common to the eastern Polynesians, at the time New Zealand was first settled.

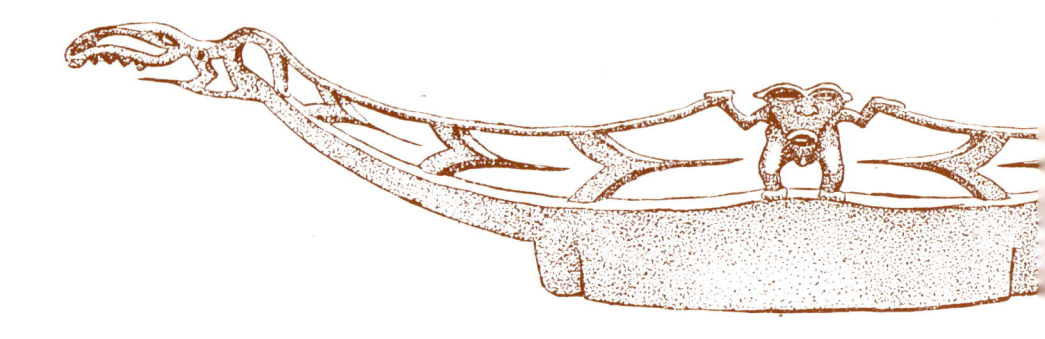

Ancient Treasures

The heritage of Maori art has worldwide recognition. Its designs and forms are instantly recognisable as the work of the Maori. Yet this was not always so distinct. The first settlers in New Zealand brought with them the art forms of Eastern Polynesia. When they landed in New Zealand they continued to make tools and decorations just as they had in the Pacific.

It is possible to compare the artefacts of other Polynesian islands about this time and find them closely related to the shapes of early Aotearoa. It was only after the Polynesians had lived some generations in New Zealand that they began to develop the art forms known now as Maori.

The sites of early settlement are sometimes identified by the kinds of implements and ornaments found there. While the Polynesians tried to make the same tools as they had in the tropical islands they were sometimes forced to use new materials. A popular breast-plate ornament was originally carved from pearl shell: in New Zealand there was no pearl shell so they laboriously worked breast-plates from stone. Tooth and reel-shaped ornaments, worn on a string about the neck, were made in New Zealand not from whale ivory but from stone or the bones of moa and seal. On the volcanic islands of Polynesia stone tools had been made from basalt. In New Zealand the Polynesians swiftly found similar rocks and worked them into similar-shaped adzes. Yet they later found other materials including greenstone which was worked into the finest adzes and weapons.

The paper mulberry, from which the tapa cloth is made in Samoa and Tonga, was introduced to New Zealand though it is now extinct. New materials for making fibre, like flax, took the place of the tropical sources such as coconut. The Polynesian settlers adapted their arts and crafts to what was available. The new materials and the new environment ultimately led to changes in the way they did things.

Early, simpler form of carving style, from collection at Auckland Institute and Museum. The carving comes from Kaitaia in Northland and is similar in style to other work from eastern Polynesia.

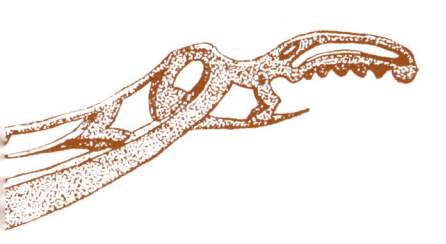

The oldest forms of decorative art have been found in Northland. They have an apparently simpler form to those objects now called Maori art. There is less decoration and the figures are similar to ancient artefacts from eastern Polynesia. Art and tools from this time are now described as Archaic, compared with the later development of Maori styles, known as Classic. It is Classic Maori art and culture which is largely remembered today.

The change from the Archaic to the Classic Maori styles may have been a gradual process. There is a series of hair combs now at Waikato Art Museum which shows a gradual change in decoration over 200 years or so. They were found in a pit at Kauri Point, Tauranga Harbour, ceremonially broken and deposited. The earliest combs were simple in design but by the end of the period several bore carvings in a more noticeably Maori style. From evidence like this it has been argued that the distinctive style of Maori carving evolved in New Zealand, as part of the process whereby the original Polynesians became the Maori people of today.

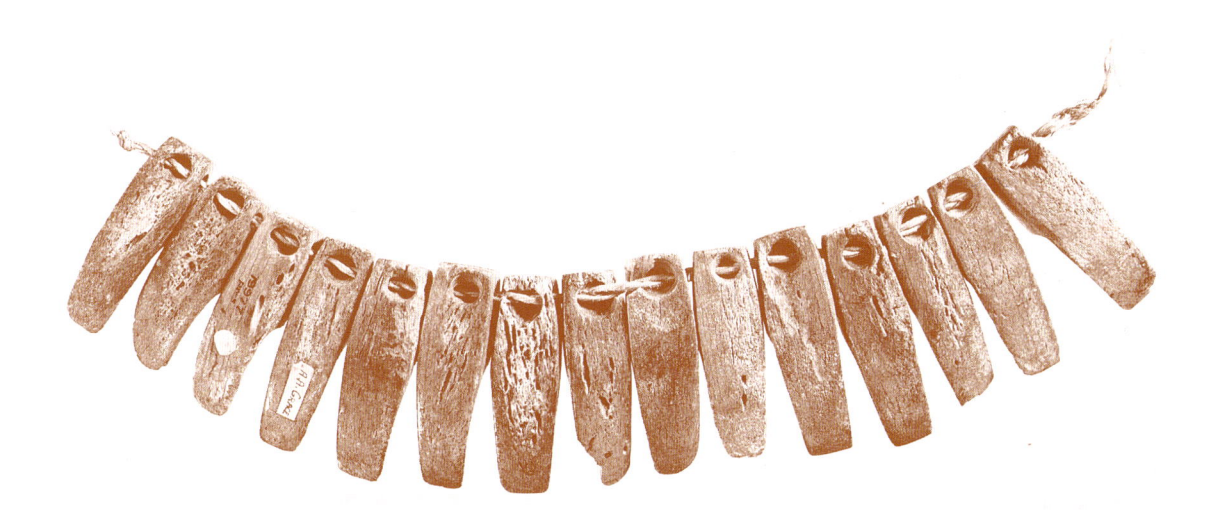

Bone necklace worked in form of teeth. The first settlers of New Zealand used local materials, like moa bone, to make artefacts in the style of their tropical homeland, where real teeth were more available.

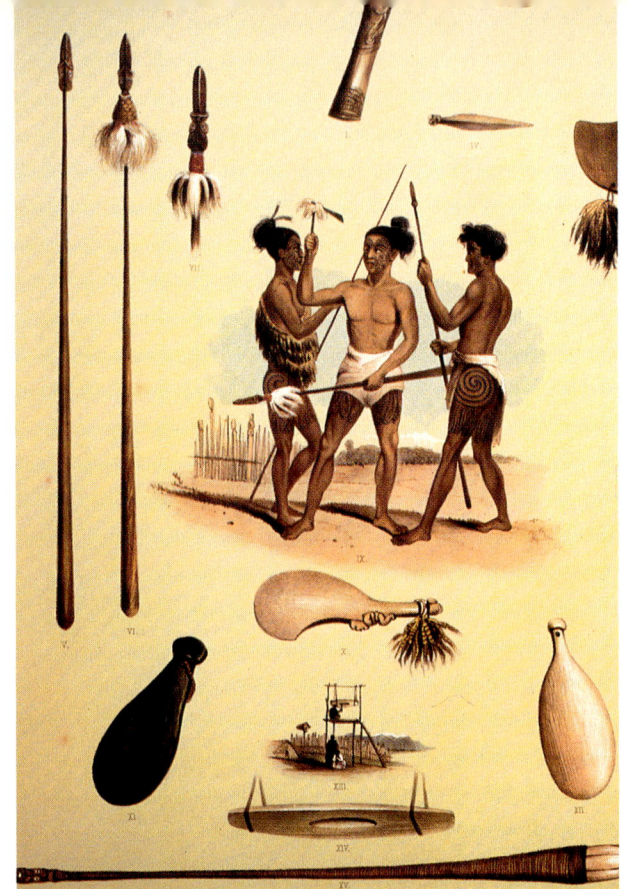

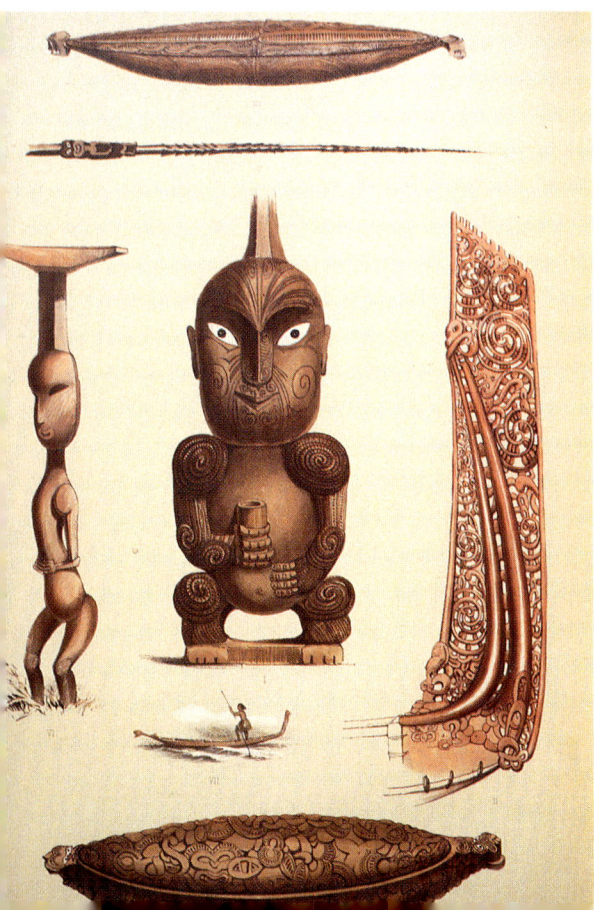

Plates from *The New Zealanders Illustrated* by George French Angas, published in 1847, show fine examples of Maori art and craft of the Classic period. Metal tools were available to carvers by the time of Angas's visit and larger carved structures were becoming more common. These plates depict weapons of war, canoe prows and decorated paddles (top left), some carved figures, a canoe stern post and storage boxes.

Classic Maori Carving & Decoration

Carved store houses or pataka (above right).

Close up of actual carving (below right) is a detail of fine work using stone chisels (shown about half actual size). Classic Maori art is, generally, highly decorative.

Classic Maori Art

The popular idea of Maori art today is the highly-decorated surfaces of the Classic carving styles. These Maori shapes, appearing too in body tattoo and decorative ornaments, are the forms that distinguish Maori art from that of the other Pacific Islands.

Maori carving is still practised today, decorating the porches and uprights of meeting houses, and in carved ornaments often sold in tourist shops. These pieces are made with modern tools of steel. It is worth remembering that many of the fine pieces to be found in museums were carved not with steel but with stone tools.

The Maori people encountered by Captain Cook's expeditions had "no sort of iron" and their fine work was accomplished with adzes and chisels worked from stone. These tools themselves, and the stone and bone ornaments and implements of the Maori, were all made with other stone tools. Maori rock quarries still exist where the "blanks" of tools were broken from the bedrock with stone "hammers". The tools were then shaped, by chipping away edges with other stones and later by a process of rubbing against harder rocks, to make surfaces smooth and edges sharp.

With such stone tools the Maori could fell trees. They could carve from them the decorations for canoe or ceremonial pole, the bargeboards of houses and food stores, and make smaller implements such as fighting clubs and digging sticks. They decorated flutes and feather boxes too.

The carvings could be surprisingly delicate despite the difficulties of working with stone chisels. The open form of a canoe prow, carved with stone tools, shows how wood could be carefully worked. A visit to a museum will show the difference between stone and steel-carved work. The stone-carved wood appears to be worked in little chips, giving the wood a bruised appearance, while steel chisels give a smoother, more flowing surface.

Variations in carving styles may be traced to different "schools" of carving, different tribes.

It has been argued that the development of the sophisticated styles of Maori art and craft began with the development of fortified villages, perhaps from the fourteenth century onwards.

The discovery that the staple sweet potato, kumara, could be grown and stored for winter food meant that less time had to be spent roaming the countryside, living off the land. In such fortunate places Maori life became more specialised. Carvers and craftspeople had a little more security, and time, in which to practise their skills.

Not every tribe had an agricultural base however. In the colder south many of the people still depended largely on seasonal journeys in search of food. On the West Coast of the South Island Maori people gathered greenstone from about 1500 A.D. and traded it with other tribes. This jade-like material was valued throughout New Zealand for ornament and weapon.

By the time of European discovery certain stronger tribes had a rich treasure of carved art. There were buildings and canoes with the faces of gods and ancestors. There were tools decorated with the symbols of their use. Men and women of status bore symbolic shapes in the form of tattoo on their bodies. They also wore cloaks with decorative patterns and body ornaments.

The Maori used wood, bone, shell and stone as substances to carve. Their favoured sculptures include a sinuous form of bird-headed figure known as a manaia and a human grotesque known as a tiki. The surfaces of such carvings are embellished often with notches and series of spirals. The simplest to see is the form of the koru, or springing fern, a symbol of life.

Most carved objects were decorated with these formal symbols. The only frequent "realistic" figure in Maori carving is the lizard, yet even on its surfaces the patterns of curve and notch are often repeated. Despite the common patterns there is a noticeable difference between the carving styles of different "schools", producing distinctive regional styles. The use of carving also varies from tribe to tribe.

Maori use of natural materials in craft and clothing are depicted here, from specimens at Auckland Institute and Museum.

At left a sample of tukutuku weaving shows the method of fabrication. The wall panel is built on a frame of raupo: flax ties are made in several patterns, each with special meanings.

Dog skin cloak uses hair of kuri, a dog species now extinct, brought to New Zealand by the Polynesian settlers. Where hair has worn away the basic materials of flax and fibre can be seen.

Maori Crafts & Decoration

Fine Maori cloaks were woven from flax fibre. Other materials were tied in to decorate. Use of coloured wool indicates these cloaks date from European times.

Kete, made from flax, are still made and used by Maori. Flax bags and gourds served as containers in a society which had no form of pottery.

CLOTHES AND FABRICS—The Wonder of Flax

Staying warm in these cold islands must have been a major problem for the Polynesians from the tropics. There they had worn little or nothing in the way of clothing. In Aotearoa an unclothed person can become chilled and die of exposure within minutes. Yet the Maori had established camps about the windswept rivermouths as far south as Southland in very early times.

It is possible they made use of the skins of seals and dogs to keep out the harsh winds which so quickly chill the body. The paper mulberry, which was a source of fabric in the tropics, could only be grown in the far north of New Zealand. Instead the Maori used flax as their main source of material for clothing and other fabrics. Fibres from the leaves of cabbage tree and kiekie were also used.

Much present knowledge of Maori clothing is drawn from the observations made by the early European explorers of New Zealand. They record the use of flax lap cloths and skirts by men and women. Skin cloaks and woven materials, embroidered with feathers, might be worn by the high born. Much of the work and fighting was done without the hindrance of clothes, apart from a small maro or apron.

Nevertheless there are many tales of people caught in exposed places and faced with death. One such records an ancestor Ngatoro-i-rangi atop Mount Tongariro, calling on his priestly sisters to send a warming fire. The progress of this fire from Hawaiki to the centre of the North Island brought a line of volcanoes and hot springs through the land, by way of White Island (Whakaari), Mt Edgecumbe (Patauaki), through Rotorua and Taupo. Maori people crossing the Southern Alps, to reach the source of greenstone in Westland, often perished on the snowfields and exposed passes.

Temporary huts built about rivermouths and hunting areas served as frequent shelters in wet and windy weather. Maori people developed ways of using the natural resources of the bush to keep warm and other tales tell of hiding in hollow trees, or recovering in hot pools. Survival demanded a profound knowledge of bushcraft. The knowledge that sticks of Kaikomako, rubbed together, made fire was an important survival skill.

The treatment and fashioning of flax was an important aid to survival for the Maori. The long, fibrous leaves sprout annually and plantations of harakeke were cultivated and carefully harvested. The plant itself was treated with reverence. When the leaves were cut away care was taken not to damage the growing point of the plant, where the fans of leaves reproduce themselves. The leaves were scraped and dried, the fibres themselves being knotted into ropes and strings, or twisted into patterns which created fabrics or panels. This form of hand-weaving could produce exceptionally fine work, flexible and hard-wearing.

Mats and cloaks might be woven, often with decorations made from dyed strands, or feathers or fur tied in. Sometimes sandals of fibre were worn.

Flax could also be tied into panels, seen today in the wall panels called tukutuku weaving, which may decorate the interiors of Maori buildings. Bulrush (raupo) can serve as framework, while kiekie and pingao are also useful fibres. The fine patterns of diamonds and other geometric shapes, all have names and symbolise natural forms.

Storage bags were important too for the Maori had no pottery. Birds might be preserved in their own fat perhaps, like "mutton-birds", enveloped in the split "leaves" of giant seaweed. Fluids might be carried in gourds or hue. The kete of flax however made a useful basket or shoulder bag, as it did a form of "disposable" plate.

The art and craft of such weaving is still carefully practised. Flax is cultivated according to the traditions and much of the finer work still makes use of the traditional dyes. Occasionally the feathers of an introduced bird, like pheasant, might replace the threatened species of native birds once used. Nevertheless the customs surrounding such creative work are still observed by traditional craftspeople.

Traditional crafts and clothing may be seen on previous pages, 32 & 33

MOKO – The Art of Tattoo

The Maori form of tattoo is known as moko. It adorns both men and women and continues the kind of carving shapes favoured by the wood workers. Spirals and the curves of the springing fern, the koru, make up the basic patterns. Moko was reserved for higher-born people and reflected their status. Women might bear only a small pattern about the chin and lips and sometimes the forehead. Many of the warriors were decorated not only on their faces, but also about the thighs and buttocks.

Tattoo were cut into the skin with tiny adzes. The dark-bluish colour of the design comes from the soot of resinous wood, or kauri gum, used to stain the wounded flesh. The cutting point of the tattoo instrument was made from bird bone, perhaps 5mm across, strapped to a handle. The process was long and painful. The pictures here come from a nineteenth-century book on moko by Major-General Robley who recorded its form at a time when many warriors still wore "the blue privilege."

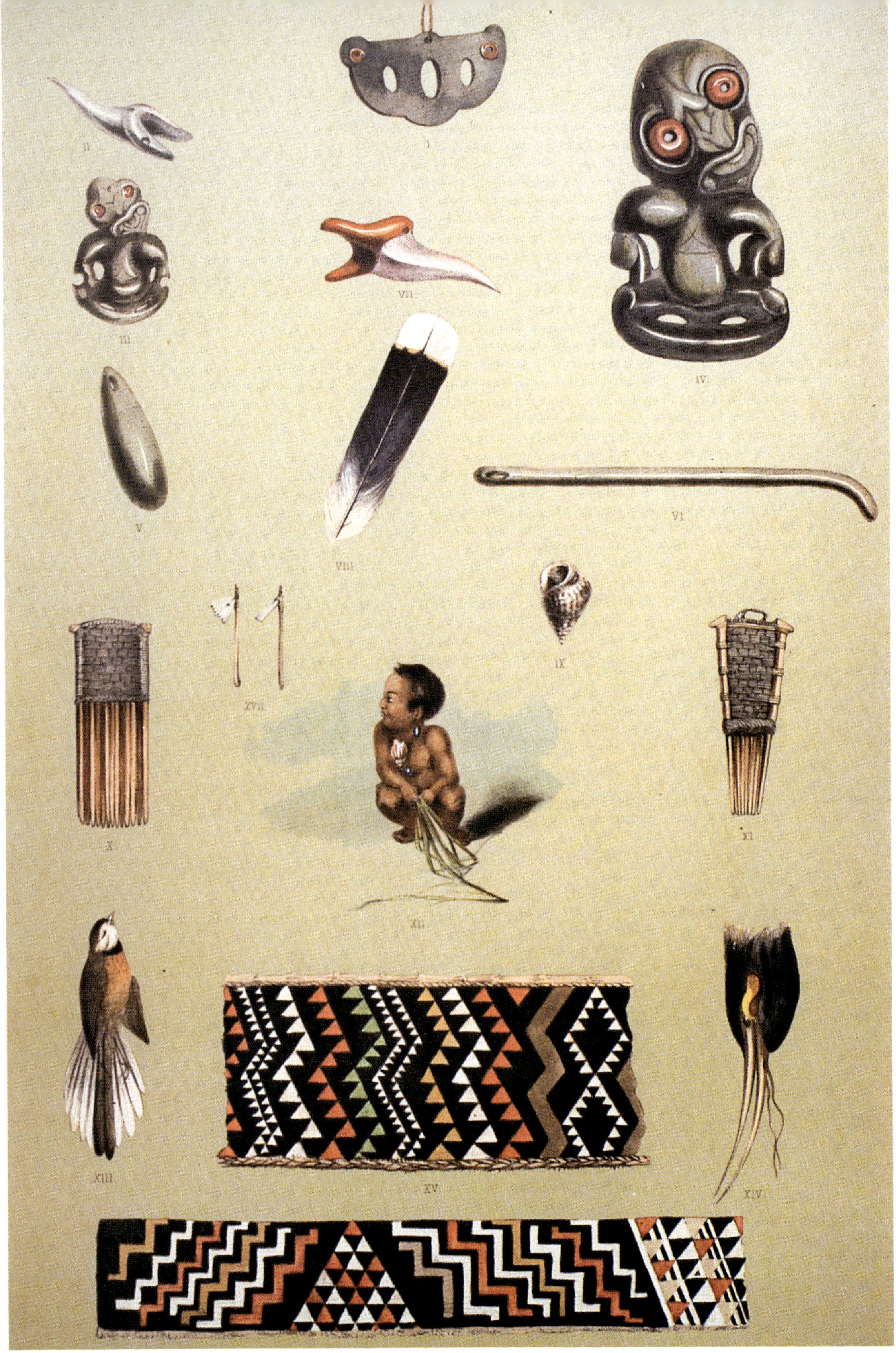

I
II
III
IV
V
VI
VII
VIII
IX
X
XI
XII
XIII
XIV
XV
XVII

MAORI ORNAMENT – Treasures take life

The decorative arts of the Maori are widely admired. From the very earliest days of Polynesian settlement ornaments were worn and tattooing practised. Reel ornaments, tooth necklaces and tattooing chisels have been found in the camps of moa-hunting Maori of the Archaic period.

The rich heritage of pendant and other forms of bodily decoration is easily seen in museums, and increasingly, at Maori functions today. The tiki is perhaps the best known, a compacted human figure, usually worked in greenstone. This form of jade comes from a few places in Westland and inland Otago, and trade in its various forms began about 1500 A.D. Greenstone was also used in the manufacture of ear pendants and other ornaments, besides its use in adzes, weapons and tools.

Other neck decorations include the whaletooth form of rei-puta, the fish-hooked hei-matua, the bat-like pekapeka and the sinuous spiral of the koropepe. Simpler pendants, kuru and kapeu, were worn round the neck, or from the ears, as were sometimes fine chisels. All these forms are still worked by artists today.

To shape them from a rock said to be harder than steel was the work of many months. Other stone, whale ivory, bone and shell were also worked. The ornaments, highly-valued, were handed down the generations. As they did they acquired their own lives, like certain weapons, gathering the mana of their successive owners and even earning names as treasures of the tribe.

Ornaments, like the tiki, were the adornments of leaders and helped give status to their wearer. Feathers of birds, such as the huia and the albatross, were also worn as a sign of high station. Sometimes the skins of birds were worn from the ear. Combs adorned the tapu head of chiefs. It was the chiefly classes too who wore the fine cloaks, with their tied in decorations of feather or skin. Bodies might be greased in animal fat or stained with earth. The most outstanding bodily decoration, however, was the tattoo or moko.

ORNAMENTS & DECORATIONS

This plate from Angas's *The New Zealanders Illustrated* *(1847)* shows typical ornaments of the Maori. Beside the more familiar tiki, worn about the neck, there are ear-rings of greenstone, including one shaped like a shark's tooth, and another of sea shell. Fantail and huia birds were also worn as ear decorations. Wooden combs held hair of warriors. Taniko weaving shows decorative edging of flax garments.

Tribes and their canoes

Without a written form of language the Maori people had no books to tell of their past. Yet they have a fine tradition of story-telling which helps to remember their history. Selected individuals became the guardians of tribal history. Families can trace their origins back over many generations by reciting their family tree or whakapapa. When missionaries in the early nineteenth century first wrote the Maori language down it provided a way to record these stories, for the first time, in books. Every story differed for each family has different lines of descent. Yet finally most Maoris trace their history back to a particular ancestor shared by other members of the tribe.

Such stories help explain the Maori tribal claims to land. They tell, usually, of the conquest of a particular territory and its taking from "the people before", the now-forgotten tribes that preceded the present ones. They tell how different parts of the tribal area were settled and by whom. They also tell of further battles and alliances, perhaps through marriage or conquest, which contribute to the family tree of present tribes. In this way some people claim membership or association with other tribes by descent. In modern times, as Maori people have moved to the cities, people of different tribes have inter-married more frequently. In the past such inter-marriage was less frequent and people tended to belong to a fiercely-independent tribe.

The story of a Maori tribe is a sacred one, for it relates people to their ancestors and their land. The tribal stories are sometimes recited with the aid of a memory stick, each nob of which represents a generation in the tribe's history. By counting back along these generations the ancestors are placed in order and the history remembered.

In other cases carvings of the ancestors serve to preserve history. The ridge pole of a meeting house may represent an ancestor, the backbone of the tribe, or sub-tribe. The wall carvings on its supporting ribs, may represent a series of ancestral figures, a kind of carved portrait gallery. Such carvings may represent relationships between tribes, through marriage, and form an alternative record of Maori history, a form of picture writing.

Maori tribal stories often begin with the journey of an ancestral canoe. The places it touches on in its journey represent claims to the land or relationships with the people who live there now. The journey from a former homeland, "Hawaiki", describes how the occupants of the present land came to possess it. Often they mention the tangata whenua, the people before, who were usually conquered or destroyed. In such cases the history of the earlier tribe is forgotten—the story of any tribal land begins with its conquest by its present occupiers. In a few

Generations of the tribe are recorded by the knobs

cases newcomers formed alliances with the tangata whenua and such tribes may retain a very long history, reaching back 35 generations or more.

By examining the various tribal stories, using dates worked out by counting back through the generations, modern historians and tribal elders have contributed to a more detailed picture of how the Maori tribes settled New Zealand. The present tribes came, some claim, from original settlements in the sub-tropical north, as these became over-populated.

Not every tribe has a founding canoe as such: some East Coast people claim they have always occupied that land. Others have put new emphasis on the canoe symbol to help them with land claims. The old land courts used sometimes to insist that the tribal story be described back to the "arrival" of a canoe. Some tribes identify their tribe as a canoe yet have traditions that tell of their wandering over land in search of new territory.

For this reason the once-popular story of the great migration of Maori people in a fleet of seven canoes to New Zealand is now discounted. The seven "founding canoes" have each a different story, and by counting back their generations it appears they in fact settled their different parts of the land over a period of 300 years or more. Modern tribes descend not from just those seven canoes. There are some 60 different canoes recorded in Maori tradition. The tribal stories also account for the formation of new tribes or sub-tribes. As populations grew, groups of people moved inland along the river valleys and lake shores and founded new tribes, or sub-tribes. Sometimes these new groups met along borders with the descendants of other "canoes" forming new alliances or enmities. The whakapapa records these links.

The map of New Zealand showing tribal boundaries was radically altered in the few years between the discovery of New Zealand by Europeans and the formation of the British colony through the Treaty of Waitangi. During the 1820s northern tribes under Hongi Hika armed themselves with European firearms and set off to conquer their traditional enemies. In a series of ferocious, cannibal raids, they decimated the tribes further south and laid claim to some of the land they conquered. Te Rauparaha made similar raids about Wellington and the South Island.

The 1820 wars between the Maori people help to explain why some tribes fought with the British, against other Maori tribes, during the later wars over land. The feelings and enmities of those days still affect Maori politics and tribal attitudes.

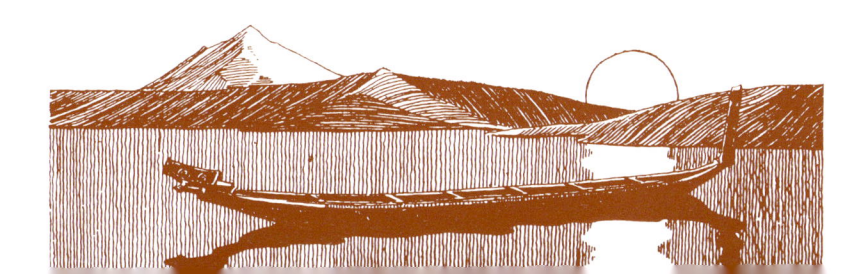

AOTEAROA—An Isolated World

Maori life developed in isolation from the ideas and ways of other countries. There were no close neighbours to borrow from. The Maori shaped their own ways of doing things.

In some areas of life they were rich in invention and imagination; the lore of nature and the spirit was complex and sophisticated to the European experience. Yet the Maori had not discovered the wheel or even the use of bow and arrow in hunting and warfare. Their method of making fire was one of the simplest.

Yet the Maori fashioned superb ornaments and tools with implements of stone. The digging stick and wooden spade were basic implements but they were often decorated in fine carving. Where other cultures continually borrowed from each other the isolated Maori people developed their own ways of coping, their own styles.

Maori "weaving" is not weaving in the sense of other cultures. Instead its methods are comparatively simple series of foldings, inter-lacing and ties. Yet the objects created could be as fine as those made by more complicated techniques.

The Maori had few material possessions beyond the ornaments of the privileged class. The artefacts that survive, however, are highly decorated even when their purpose was functional.

Over their centuries in New Zealand the Maori changed the design of their canoes to match new needs. Only a few double-hulled canoes were reported by European discoverers, though this was the pattern once used to conquer the oceans. Instead the Maori built long, single-hulled canoes which could penetrate the rivers and narrower waterways of Aotearoa.

After the introduction of European materials, such as iron, the Maori people rapidly adjusted their techniques. These changes were sometimes beneficial, like the introduction of new food crops such as the potato, and at other times disastrous as with the musket. The process of borrowing ideas and skills from neighbouring countries, which had helped the continental peoples advance through the centuries, were in Aotearoa accomplished in just a few years from that first contact with Europe.

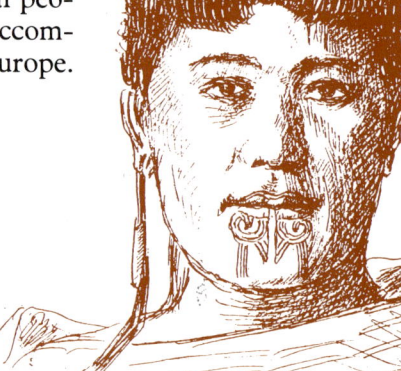